The ANZAC Hospital No. 1 at Harefield and the Australians who died there and elsewhere but who are buried at Harefield

1914-1918

Tanya Britton

ISBN

978-0-99927922-2-0

INTRODUCTION

At the beginning of the War, Australian casualties were admitted to British hospitals but as the War progressed it was thought that the Australians should have their own hospitals and by October 1916 three such hospitals had been established. The first was Harefield Park. This is the history of the hospital, taken from 'Harefield during the First World War 1914-1918'. Also included is a list of the Australians who died whilst at the hospital. However, not all the casualties listed below died at the Anzac Hospital at Harefield, although all but one is buried at Harefield. In those cases where the serviceman died elsewhere, this has been mentioned in the text.

Hillingdon Local Studies, Archives and Museum Service has kindly allowed me to make use of their photographs. However, where this is not the case, the source is mentioned in the text.

THE ANZAC HOSPITAL No. 1 at HAREFIELD PARK

Harefield Park and its estate of 250 acres was owned by a wealthy Australian from New South Wales - Mr. Charles Billyard-Leake and his wife, Letitia. They offered it to the Australian Ministry of Defence as a convalescent home where officers, warrant officers, NCOs and men of the A.I.F. would recuperate after illness or injury.

The Hospital (Hillingdon Local Studies, Archives and Museum Service)

It was also to act as a depot for collecting invalids for return to Australia. The property was on three storeys with outbuildings, lakes, shrubberies, flower gardens and paddocks. This offer was accepted in December 1914, and within a month the Australian MOD had approved staff - one captain, one sergeant, one corporal, four men as wardsmen and orderlies, one matron and five nursing sisters. Ethel Gray, an Australian Queen Alexandra Nurse from Melbourne was specifically selected for the job and proceeded to England, with five nurses, arriving on 26[h] March 1915. She found the house still containing much of the original furniture and carpets, which had to be removed. The Billyard-Leakes moved into Black Jack's Mill.

Hospital entrance (Hillingdon Local Studies, Archives and Museum Service)

At the beginning of the War Australian casualties had been admitted to British hospitals but by October 1916 three auxiliary hospitals had been established. The first hospital - No. 1 Australian Auxiliary Hospital was in Harefield and was opened in 1915. This was followed by the second at Southall, at a large school built in 1858 to educate the poor children of the Parish of St. Marylebone, whi ch held as many as 800 Australian patients and staff, and which eventually specialised in the fitting of artificial limbs. The third was at Dartford in the Orchard Hospital at Long Reach, which at the time of the commencement of the war was unused. Smaller hospitals were also established at Welwyn where there were 24 beds and at Moreton Gardens, Kensington with 40 beds.

Wards at the hospital (Hillingdon Local Studies, Archives and Museum Service)

Harefield had a complement of 26 medical officers and 112 other ranks, 26 sisters, 36 staff nurses, 120 Australian VAD nurses seconded from British hospitals and 6 masseuses. Many local people also volunteered to help. Eleven NCOs and men of the Australian Medical Transport Corps, seven ambulances, two touring cars, one motor lorry and one motorcycle carried out evacuation from Denham Station. The speed that some of these vehicles travelled at was far too fast and complaints were made. By 1917 the road between the hospital and Denham was in a deplorable state of disrepair.

Originally it was estimated that the house would accommodate 50 soldiers in winter and 150 during the spring-summer. Hutted wards would have to be built on the front lawn. Ethel Gray had almost six weeks to get everything ready. By May, 80 beds were ready. The first commanding officer and five orderlies who were sailing on the troopship '*Runic*' were due mid May. In May 1915 arrangements were being made to extend the accommodation to 500 beds. Australian and New Zealand troops who had mostly fought at Gallipoli were expected. The first patients (7 of them) arrived via Lemnos and Malta on 2nd June 1915.

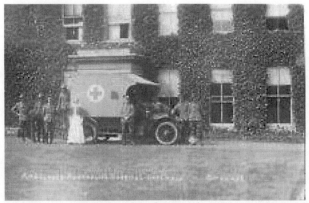

Ambulance outside the hospital (Hillingdon Local Studies, Archives and Museum Service)

On 17th June more wounded arrived. This made a total of 80 patients. Huts were put up all over the place - most where the cricket pitches had been. A mortuary was situated beyond the kitchen garden. By 22nd June the hospital had 170 patients, two weeks later there were 362. The Harefield Asbestos Works offered to convert a bay windowed room into an operating theatre and on 9th July the first operation was carried out.

In the first week of January 1916 the first patients were evacuated to Australia. The first death occurred just over one month later when on 8th February 1916 Robert Sidney Wake, 5th Battalion Australian Infantry, who was born at Cullercoats,

Northumberland, died of wounds. He was in his early 20s and was buried at St. Mary's Church, Harefield, as are all that died here.

At first the practice was that wounded Australians on their arrival in England would proceed to one or other of the many British General Military Hospitals and when well enough they would be transferred to Harefield. It was soon realised that with the enormity of casualties, it should become a fully equipped hospital.

Recuperating Australian servicemen at Harefield out for a stroll (WILSON, The Great War)

In mid to late May 1916, the number of patient dropped to about 100, but quickly rose to 500 as a result of the men wounded in France. By now, there was accommodation at the hospital for about 960 casualties. By October 1916 it became a hospital - the Australian Auxiliary Hospital No. 1 - with increased medical and nursing personnel. An artificial limb workshop opened in December 1915 and an eye, ear and throat ward in January 1916. At the end of 1916 Ethel Gray was posted to France and was succeeded by Matron Gould who in turn was replaced by Miss Ross in November 1917.

Lady Coglan and Lady Talbot by the bedside of a wounded Australian. The photograph was taken during a garden party in the grounds of the hospital. (WILSON, The Great War)

The hospital gradually developed into a specialist centre for radiography and electrotherapeutic services, with 43 wards. By the end of the War accommodation had increased to 1,000 beds by the erection of further huts and other types of speciality treatment had evolved for eye, ear, and nose and throat conditions.

When the hospital opened supplies of food were arranged through the Army Service Corps (ASC) at Hounslow. In November 1915 a committee was formed to purchase all foods on the open market. Colletts General Stores at Harefield supplied the bread. The produce of the farm, usually despatched to London, was also used for supplying the hospital. Tenders were invited for the supply of fresh milk, which by mid 1917 had grown to 143 gallons every four months. In early 1918 an acre was given over to grow foodstuffs as part of the allotment scheme. The main kitchen situated in the house, was relieved by a field kitchen in the grounds constructed before mid 1915.

The King and Queen, attended by the Countess of Minto and Captain B. Godfrey-Faussett, RN, visited the 1st Australian Auxiliary Hospital on 16th August 1915 for two hours, and in the same month a sentry box was placed at the entrance. The Australian Prime Minister also visited the hospital as did other leading Australians. In the Spring of 1917, the Duke of Connaught presented several medals for gallant service in France and Gallipoli.

The 'Long Ramp' was the main thoroughfare. It was an open board walk which started under a big oak tree and joined to other covered ways. It was busy most days with men arriving or departing and also gave good protection in the winter months.

The casualties wore a light blue uniform with a red tie whilst in hospital, but once they were well enough to venture outside they also wore a blue band on their arm. Londoners called this 'the blue badge of courage'.

A great deal of thought went into the providing recreational facilities for them. For instance, Harefield Park Boomerang was the magazine of the No. 1 Australian Auxiliary Hospital, Harefield, which was started in December 1916 by Pte. C.A.Evenden and Pte. H.J. Kemp and afterwards controlled by a committee. In 1917 a band was organised. Patients undertook fancy work which was exhibited and sports days were also held. A patients' canteen was opened and put under the control of the Director of recreation and study and an Orderlies

Canteen opened for all ranks below Sergeant. By early 1918, the canteen had made healthy profits and these were used to decorate the Recreation Hall. A large stove was also provided and two pianos. The Breakspear Institute, which had a very small extension built in late 1915, was also greatly used by the wounded Australians.

Many invitations for outings were extended to the wounded men, but the shortage of transport was a problem, especially in November 1917 when there were as many as 1,100 patients being treated in the hospital. Fortunately many of the locals rallied round to help.

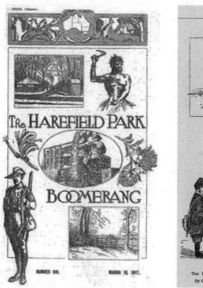 

Front and back pages from 'The Boomerang'
(Hillingdon Local Studies, Archives and Museum Service)

There were no reports of antisocial behaviour on the part of the Australians at Harefield, apart from the occasional pilfering and once an actual assault on a girl, unlike the wounded and recuperating Australian soldiers and some staff from the temporary military hospital situated at Southall who had been banned from Southall park for most of the war because of their bad behaviour, mainly when they had been drinking, and very late in the war were also banned from all the public houses in Southall, although it had been made illegal to sell intoxicants to a member of His Majesty's Forces who was undergoing hospital treatment. Southall Council also imposed a 10pm curfew on them. However, some boys had tried to smuggle alcoholic drinks into the hospital for the wounded men but were caught and severely reprimanded.

In 1916, Private J. Naughton 3rd Battalion 'D'Coy Australian Expeditionary Force, a badly wounded patient wrote, under the title of 'My Short Career', a short record of his service – 'I enlisted August 26th 1914, left Australia on October 19th 1914, landed in Egypt on December 3rd 1914, left Egypt on April 2nd 1915, for the Dardanelles, landed Gallipoli Peninsula on April 25th 1915, wounded at Lone Pine on August 14th 1915 – result both hands blown off and badly wounded in right leg'. It was a perfectly legible account, written with a pen secured between his wrists.

An incident which caused much sadness to the patients was when Jimmy the kangaroo, the hospital mascot, was shot dead in May 1918 by a local farmer who had no idea what sort of animal it was. Jimmy had been presented to one of the volunteer workers in October 1916 by the daughter of

Sir William Birdwood, General Officer Commanding the ANZACs. It was Sir William himself who had first thought of the word ANZAC when asked to supply a handy telegraphic address in 1915. Another mascot, a cockatoo, would imitate the sound of a 'Turkish shell'.

Another view of the hospital (Hillingdon Local Studies, Archives and Museum Service)

Reveille was at 6am. Fall In was heard at 6.15am followed by half an hour of exercises then followed by breakfast. Sick Parade and lectures took place in the morning and after dinner a march or some other exercise was obligatory which lasted until 4pm. After tea the rest of the day was free. First Post was at 9. 30pm, Last Post 10.00pm and Lights Out half an hour later.

The hospital was open to visitors on Wednesday, Saturday and Sunday between 2pm and 5.30pm It did not treat officers, instead they were cared for at 1 Moreton Gardens, The Boltons, Kensington, remaining a Casualty Clearing Depot throughout the war. At Harefield, altogether over fifty buildings were erected, forty-three of which were used for the reception of patients. In 1916 when the house was full, Mr. Billyard-Leake offered for rent the 'Red House by the Strolleys' in Park Lane opposite the Officers' Mess.

Thousands of wounded Australian soldiers passed through, one source estimates 49,000 wounded Australians passed through the hospital, but it maybe as many as 100,000 and in nine months in 1917 there were 10,232 admissions. The largest number of patients at any one time was 970. 111 soldiers died, including at least one suicide, and one nursing sister, Ruby Dickinson from Sydney, died of influenza in the Sisters' hospital in the afternoon of 23rd June 1918. She had been at Harefield since January 1918, having previously been nursing in a number of hospitals in France. A Union Jack was borrowed from Harefield Council School to cover the coffins of those that died at the hospital and it was lent for the duration of the War. Early in 1917 a fund was started for the erection of headstones to all the graves.

In January 1919, 72 patients were admitted and 691 discharged. At the same time Woodlands, which had been taken over in March 1918 after standing empty for some time, and Cranfield House, Harefield, which had been the quarters of the Women's VAD at the hospital were vacated. When the institution closed the remaining patients were transferred to Weymouth.

Immediately after the war Harefield Park house was purchased by the Council and became a tuberculosis sanatorium in 1921. It was considered to be the finest and most up-to-date sanatorium in England. The north wards were constructed during World War Two for use by the Emergency Medical

Services. It later became part of the world-renowned Harefield Hospital.

THE WAR MEMORIAL

The unveiling and dedication of the war memorial placed in the Churchyard of St. Mary's Church to the memory of the Australian soldiers who died in hospital at Harefield took place on Sunday 13th November 1921 at 3.15pm. The Archbishop of Melbourne dedicated the granite obelisk and the unveiling ceremony was performed by the Agent-Generals of Western Australia and Tasmania, and Sir Ross Smith, an airman who flew with his brother from England to Australia. The cemetery is entered through an archway of Portland stone. A map of the cemetery is in St. Mary's Church and shows the location of the graves.

A 'wheel', signed by all of those Australians who remained in the hospital after war ended, can be found in Uxbridge Local Studies Library.

On 28th April 1929, a marble tablet placed at the western end of the nave, in memory of the 112 Australian soldiers buried in Harefield Churchyard, presented to the Church by Sir Francis Newdigate, GCMG, patron of the living, was unveiled by Major-General the Hon. Sir Granville de Laune Kyrie, KCMG,CB, High Commissioner of Australia.

In April 1950, the Australian Chapel of Remembrance was dedicated by the Lord Bishop of London, the service of which was broadcast by the BBC to Australia and New Zealand at the Annual Commemoration of Anzac Day at Harefield Church. Following the dedication, the Lord Lieutenant of the County, Lord Latham, unveiled a plaque inscribed:

This chapel is dedicated to the Glory of God and to the memory of the men and women of Australia fighting forces who gave their lives in the cause of freedom, 1914-18, 1939-1945'. Also in that year, the flag which flew over the Australian Hospital during the 1914-1918 war was presented to St. Mary's Church and hangs in the memorial chapel.

ABBERTON, Edmund
Born in Manchester (or Perth, Western Australia), enlisted at Perth on 8th January 1916, embarked at Melbourne on 25th May 1916 and sailed on the troopship HMAT *'Ascanius'*. 10831, Sapper, 3rd Div. Signal Coy., Australian Engineers. He was on leave in London when he was taken ill with influenza and admitted to the hospital, where he died from pneumonia on 6th November 1918. He had been a telegraphist. Son of Michael and Martha Abberton of Railway Terrace, West Guildford, Western Australia.

ADKINS, Charles
Born at Perth, Western Australia, enlisted at Perth on 20th March 1916. He embarked at Fremantle on 13th October 1916, sailing on HMAT *'Suffolk'*. 5791, Private, 28th Battalion, Australian Infantry. Charles was wounded by shrapnel in the head and elbow at Bullecourt during terrible and desperate fighting at the battle of Arras. The attack had begun on 12th April 1917 in bitterly cold and snowy weather and extended until the end of May. It was directed against the line at a point between Bullecourt village on the left and Lagnicourt on the right. Its objective had been to hold and use up as many enemy divisions as possible in order to help the French offensive on the Marne which was about to start in the south. He was taken to the 6th Australian Field Ambulance on 25th April 1917 and admitted to 13th Stationary Hospital on 4th May 1917, then to the Royal Herbert Hospital, Woolwich and later to the hospital, where he died of a cerebral abscess on 5th June 1917, aged 24 or 25. Son of Charles and Margaret Adkins of 170 Carr Street, Leederville, Western Australia. He had been a loco fireman.

ALFORD, Roy Hensley
Enlisted at Sunshine, Victoria. 8023, Acting Bombardier, 16th Bty., AFA Brigade, Australian Field Artillery. Roy had been admitted to the hospital on 20th October 1918, where he died of influenza on 30th October 1918, aged 21. Son of Robert Henry and Mary Stewart of Graham Street, Sunshine, Victoria, Australia.

ANDERSON, Alfred Alexander
Born at Thursday Island, Queensland, enlisted at Townsville, Queensland on 26th June 1916. 3440, Private, 41st (Queensland) Battalion, Australian Infantry.

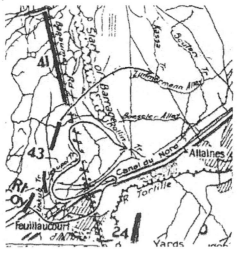

Allaines and the Tortille flats (Bean, C.E.W. Official history of Australia in the war of 1914-1918)

He had been wounded on 1st September 1918 during the ANZAC's greatest battle on the Western Front at Mont St. Quentin as the 41st Queenslanders, the centre battalion, attacked a frontage of 1,000 yards. The 41st Queenslanders had assembled at the Bapaume road and hurried to catch the creeping barrage which fell beyond some of the German trenches and was also noticeably thin. They were in a sharp fight and during the seizure of their first objective came under terrific machine-gun fire from the country ahead, especially from the Franz Regiment at Allaines. By a second fight the leading companies seized Yassa and Kassa Trenches, slightly short of their first objective. A pause in the attack gave the enemy time to rally in Scutari and Broussa Trenches. The 41st had to descend downhill and break through to this line but on reaching the gully the left company was shot at direct by batteries on the Tortille flats and machine-guns in copses on the flanks. The fiercest fire ever experienced had been encountered by the southern company of the 41st and the advance stopped. However, all along the line was victorious. Rawlinson captured 3,500 prisoners at Peronne and the French vigorously progressed in Coucy forest. He died at the hospital on 5th October 1918, aged 21. The post-mortem showed that he died from diabetes and coma. He had been a carpenter.

ANDERSON, William Leith
Born in Scotland, enlisted at Brisbane on 28th August 1915. 1464, Driver, 5th Div. Ammunition Col. Australian Field Artillery. Will died of pneumonia at the hospital on 8th February 1917, aged 31 (or 33). He had been a carpenter.

ARMSTRONG, Ernest George
Ernest enlisted at Colac, embarking for service abroad at Adelaide on 11th January 1916, sailing on

HMAT 'Borda'. He was serving as 18792, Private, 29th Battalion, Australian Infantry, AIF. He died of tuberculosis of the lungs on 21st November 1917, aged 23. He had been a wood carver. Son of John and Mary Ann Armstrong of Colac, Victoria, Australia.

AUSTIN, William John
William was born at Hamilton, Victoria. On 10th September 1914 he enlisted at Murrumbeena, Victoria. At the time of his death he was serving as 1033, Sergeant, Australian Imp. Force HQ. He was admitted to the hospital on 7th October 1918, suffering from influenza and died on 11th October 1918 (as shown on his death certificate). The CWGC gives his date of death as 11th November 1918. Husband of G. Austin of Wornack Road, Murrumburra, Victoria, Australia. He had been a commercial traveller.

BARNES, Keith
Keith enlisted at Sydney, NSW on 7th November 1916, serving as 2820, Private, 33rd Battalion, Australian Infantry, AIF. He died of tuberculosis from which he had suffered for 3 months and 18 days on 14th June 1917, aged 21. He had been a motor driver. Son of John William and Louisa Maud Barnes.

BARTLETT, Joseph
Joe was born at 16 Norwich Court, Fetter Lane, London in about 1880, enlisted at Melbourne on 11th November 1915, embarking at Sydney on 17th December 1915 on HMAT 'Berrima'. He served as 5428, Sapper, 12th Field Company Engineers Regiment, AIF. He was reported to have died of

malignant endocarditis on 13th April 1919, aged 39. A post mortem was carried out which shows that he died on 12th April 1919 at No.3 Australian Hospital at Dartford from ulcerative endocarditis (syphilitic) from which he had suffered for five months and double terminal lobar pneumonia. Son of William James and Emily Bartlett; husband of Emily Marietta Bartlett of 99 Duncan Buildings, Gray's Inn Road, Holborn, London. He had previously been an ornamental tile fixer.

BASSETT, Leslie John
Leslie enlisted at Duntroon, embarked at Sydney on 11th March 1916 on HMAT '*Orsova*'. He was a Private in the 32nd Battalion, Australian Infantry, AIF, with 4312 (4712) as his regimental number. He died of a tubercle lung on 10th January 1919, aged 37. He had been a steward. Son of Henry James and Sarah Bassett of 39 Stamford Road, Kingsland, London, England.

BAUFOOT, James Cornelius
James was born at Madras in India, enlisted at Menindie on 15th July 1915, embarked at Adelaide on HMA Transport '*Benalla*' on 27th October 1915. 3544, Private, 50th Battalion, Australian Infantry. He had been a motor mechanic and was accidentally killed (dislocation of spine) at the 1st Australian Auxiliary Hospital, Harefield Park, on 30th June 1918, aged 25. The cause of death was stated as 1) fracture dislocation spine and 2) Pyelonephritis.

BICE, John Gilbert
John was born at Inglewood, Victoria, Australia, where he enlisted on 20th September 1916, having

previously been a labourer. He embarked on HMAT *'Shropshire'* at Melbourne on 25th September 1916, serving as 2187, Private, 37th Battalion, Australian Infantry. He died of tuberculosis of the lungs on 25th May 1917, aged 20. His brother, Herbert, serving with the 50th Australian Infantry, was killed in action near Ypres during the Battle of Messines on 9th June 1917. They had been in brought into action unknown to the Germans, from the Bullecourt zone to near Wytschaete on 7th June 1917 but a dangerous gap had been left in which a party of Germans with machine-guns remained entrenched for two days. On 9th June 1917 the 50th and 52nd Australian Infantry carried the place by storm. They were the sons of Luke Edward and Lillian Bice.

BLAKE, Richard Charles
Richard was born at Camberwell, Victoria, Australia, where he enlisted on 27th October, 1915. He embarked on HMAT *'Wiltshire'* at Melbourne on 7th March 1916 as a Private in the 7th Battalion, Australian Infantry, later transferring to 4733, Private, Australian Cycle Corps, AIF. He died of pneumonia on 2nd November 1918, aged 26. He had been a farmer (or a kitchenman in a mental hospital at Kew, Victoria). Son of Richard Charles and Annie Blake.

BONE, Gordon Walter
Gordon was born at Willesden, London, in 1888, enlisted at Subiaco, Western Australia. 3012, Driver, 4th Div., MT Coy., Australian Army Service Corps. He was admitted to the hospital very ill, where he died of influenza at 9.45, on 28th October 1918, aged 30. Son of the late Walter, who died in 1915 and

Alice Bone; husband of Bertha E. Bone of Broxbourne, Shaftesbury, Burwood, Sydney, Australia. He was at first a butcher but later became a salesman.

BRADFORD, Clement Everly, MM and Bar
Clem had enlisted at Murray Bridge on 28th May 1915, embarking at Adelaide on HMAT *'Star of England'* on 21st September 1915. At the time of his death he was serving as 2730, Sergeant, 50th Battalion, Australian Infantry, AIF. Died of heart failure on 12th October 1918, aged 22. He had at one time been a shop assistant. Son of Francis John and Julia Sarah Bradford of Murray Bridge, South Australia.

BUCKNALL, Guy
Guy was born in Majorca, the son of Guy and Isabel Bucknall, enlisted at Cotswold, Victoria, Australia on 10th May 1916. He embarked at Melbourne on the troopship HMS *'Ulysses'* on 25th October 1916. At the time of his death he was serving as 527, Air Mechanic 2nd class, 69 Squadron, Australian Flying Corps. The Squadron was formed in September 1916 in Egypt, from personnel from No. 1 Australian Squadron and Light Horse in that area. On 28th December 1916 the Squadron arrived at South Carlton in Lincolnshire for training before going to France, using a variety of aircraft. He was admitted to the 4th Northern Hospital in Lincoln on 4th March 1917 and discharged but was readmitted on 14th June 1917 very ill with pleurisy and influenza. As he was not recovering, arrangements were made to invalid him back to Australia, but he was sent to Harefield as

a stretcher case, where he died of peritonitis on 4th December 1917, aged 22.

CLARKE, Walter Allen

Walter had enlisted at Moree, NSW., on 16th January, 1917, serving as 6534, Private, 18th Battalion, Australian Infantry of the 5th Brigade. He had been wounded in France at Ville-sur-Ancre in an advance on Morlancourt on 19th May 1918. Two companies of the 18th Battalion had carried out the main attack with a platoon of a third company having been sent out to form a strong-post where the right flank rested and its three other platoons serving as carrying parties. The

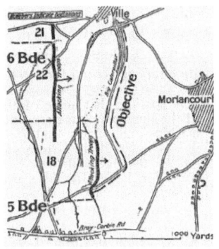

fourth company did not advance.

Morlacourt (Bean, C.E.W. Official history of Australia in the war of 1914-1918)

The attack had been designed partly to shorten the line with a view to saving troops and partly to deal the Germans a blow from a favourable position. He died of pneumonia on 29th April 1919.

CLEMENTS, Frederick

Fred was born in London in about 1889. He served as 2612, Private, 12th Battalion, Australian Infantry,

AIF. He embarked at Fremantle for service abroad on 26th September 1915, sailing on HMAT *'Anchises'*. He was wounded at Passchendaele at the Third Battle of Ypres in the late summer to early autumn of 1917 and as a result had his left leg amputated and died from primary enipyema and secondary sepsis on 28th March 1918, aged 28. Son of Henry and Jane Clements of 62 High Street, Colliers Wood, Merton, England. He had been a hotel attendant.

CLIFFORD, Harry William
Harry was born at Gravesend, Kent, enlisted at Surrey Hills, VIC., on 26th June 1916, embarked on HMAT *'Nestor'* at Melbourne on 2nd October 1916. He was a Private in the 58th Battalion, Australian Infantry with 2626 as his regimental number. He died at the No. 3 Australian Auxiliary Hospital, The Orchard, Dartford on 3rd June 1919, aged 40 or 41. A post-mortem was carried out which revealed that he died of malignant disease of the stomach and pancreas (sarcoma) and exhaustion Son of John William and Mary Frances Clifford; husband of Mary Hannah Clifford of 22 Lorne Parade, Surrey Hills, Victoria, Australia. He had gone to Australia when he was about 18 and was a miner.

CLOVER, William Crellin
William enlisted at Drouin on 26th July 1915, embarked at Melbourne on the troopship HMAT *'Hororata'* on 27th September 1915. 1233, Trooper, 2nd or 4th Australian Light Horse, AIF. He was taken ill in about June 1916 and died of tuberculosis of the lungs on 23rd June 1917, aged 25. Son of Daniel and Maud Mary Clover of Drouin, Gippsland, Victoria, Australia.

CONNOR, Roy

Roy was born at Wellington, New South Wales, enlisted at Wellington on 7th September 1915, serving as 3047, Private, 4th Battalion, Australian Infantry. He died of tubercular meningitis and a tubercle lung on 29th April 1918, aged 25. Son of James and Jane Connor of 38 Great Buckingham Street, Redfern, Sydney. He had been a baker. Buried: St. Mary's Church, Harefield.

COOKESLEY, Clifford

Born in South Melbourne, Australia, Clifford enlisted at Perth, WA., on 17th August 1914 as 17, Private, 11th Battalion, Australian Infantry, AIF. He was being treated in the Kitchener Military Hospital at Brighton (at some time serving as the workhouse there), where he had been since 17th March 1918, but was transferred to Harefield on 26th March 1918 where he died of a brain tumour at 9.55pm on 28th February 1917, aged 17 or 21. Son of John Moore Cookesley and Margaret Jane Cookesley. He had been a gardener.

COPTON, William

William was born at Melbourne, Australia, enlisted at Melbourne on 19th November 1914. He served as 1440, Private, 8th Battalion, Australian Infantry, AIF. He was admitted to the hospital on 1st August 1918, suffering from acute yellow fever atrophy in the liver and died there on 19th August 1918, aged 26. Son of William Copton; husband of M. Copton of 88 Kennington Road, Lambeth, England. He had been a carpenter.

DALE, Joseph John

Joseph was born at Brunswick, Victoria. He embarked on the troopship HMAT *'Ascanius'* at Melbourne on 27th May 1916, serving as 642, Private, 39th Battalion, Australian Infantry, AIF. He died of primary pneumonia on 27th June 1918, aged 29. Son of Joseph William and Ann Bridges Dale of 'Grandview', Coleraine, Victoria, Australia. He was a builder and contractor, and carpenter, and a partner in the firm of Dale & Sons.

DENNIS, John Williams Howard

John was born at Geelong, Victoria, enlisted at Clare, SA., on 27th July 1916 and embarked on HMAT *'Nestor'* at Melbourne on 2nd October 1916. 5813, Private, 23rd Battalion, Australian Infantry, AIF. He was wounded in the leg at Bullecourt in an attack on German defenses near Arras between 9th April and 16th May 1917. He was admitted to the hospital at some time, where he committed suicide by cutting his throat whilst of temporarily unsound mind on 7th March 1918, aged 46. He had only been at Harefield a few days and was shortly to return to Australia. Prior to enlisting he had been arrested on a charge of murder but had been acquitted in Australia. Son of John William and Sarah J. Dennis; husband of Eliza Florence Dennis of 'Marola', Trentham Street, Sandringham, Victoria, Australia. He had been a farmer (station manager).

DICKINSON, Ruby Droma

Miss Dickinson was born at Forbes, New South Wales. She enlisted at Sydney on 11th July 1917, leaving Australia on 20th July the same year. After some time at the general hospital on Lemnos Isle she went to France to nurse at a number of hospitals there. She came to the ANZAC hospital in January 1918 as Staff Nurse, Australian Army Nursing Service. She died of influenza on 23rd June 1918, aged 32. Daughter of William and Julia Dickinson of 'Arizona', Almora Street, Mosman, Queensland.

DINES, Charles Stewart
Born at Baan Baa, New South Wales, Charles enlisted at Unanderra, NSW on 6th January 1916, embarked on HMAT '*Beltana*' at Sydney on 13th May 1916. 74, Lance-Cpl., 36th Battalion, Australian Infantry, AIF. He died of sarcoma at Harefield on 4th April 1917, aged 21. He had been a carpenter apprentice. Son of Thomas Smith Wilton Dines and Emily Dines of Thornleigh, New South Wales.

DOBSON, Frederick
3428, Civilian Australian Munition Worker (Engineer's Fitter). Died at No. 3 Australian Auxiliary Hospital at Dartford on 8th May 1919. The Post Mortem showed he died from chronic tuberculosis (lungs and adrenals) from which he had suffered for 10 months and Addison's Disease. He was 42 years old.

DUDDLE, William Colbert
Will enlisted at Goulburn, NSW on 19th November 1914, embarked at Sydney on 6th February 1915, on HMAT '*Clan Maccorquadale*', serving as 781, Private, 'D' Coy., 15 Platoon, 56th Battalion, Australian Infantry. William was wounded in the side, right arm and eye by a shell at Louveral, near Polygon Wood, while holding the line on 28th-29th October 1917. He was taken unconscious to the 14th

Casualty Clearing Station at 'the Mound', sent to England and admitted to the Military Hospital at Colchester. He was transferred to Harefield on 15th November 1917 and died of shell wounds to his head and meningitis from which he had suffered for 3 months on 28th December 1917, aged 25. He had been a labourer (groom). Son of Mrs. E. Duddle of 106 Grafton Street, Goulburn, New South Wales.

DYNES, Terrence William, MM
Terrence enlisted at Richmond Victoria on 14th February 1916, embarking at Melbourne on 4th April 1916 on the troopship HMAT *'Euripides'*. He was serving as 4679, Private, 23rd Battalion, Australian Infantry, AIF. He died from broncho-pneumonia on 29th October 1918. He had been awarded the Military Medal in about 1918.

EASTHAM, Herbert James
Herbert enlisted at Collingwood, VIC., on 5th February 1917, embarking on HMAT *'Shropshire'* at Melbourne on 11th May 1917, serving as 3546 (or 3565 or 3564), Private, 2nd Battalion, Australian Pioneers., AIF. He died from syncope and purulent bronchitis influenza on 30th November 1918, aged 26. Husband of Mrs. C.M. Eastham of George Street, Echuca, New South Wales. He had been a motor driver.

ELLIOTT, Ernest Robert
Ernest had enlisted at Tee Tree Gully, SA., on 20th May 1915, and embarked on RMS *'Mongolia'* at Adelaide on 9th March 1916. 4767, Private, 1st Australian Auxiliary Hospital Australian Army Medical Corps. During a storm at Rickmansworth,

he and another Australian were cycling in the opposite direction but collided. He was thrown from his bike and fractured his skull. He died shortly afterwards of these injuries at the hospital on 9th September 1918 at about 6.30 in the evening, aged 25. He had been a labourer. Son of Walter George and Emily Jane Ashby Elliott of Tea Tree Gully, South Australia.

ELLIOTT, Michael
Michael was born at Delmy, Ross-shire, Scotland, enlisted at Frankston, VIV., on 3rd January 1916, serving as 4412, Private, 24th Battalion, Australian Infantry, AIF. Died of tuberculosis of the lungs on 7th February 1918, aged 23. He had been a nurseryman. Son of the late John and Margaret Jane Elliott. He had gone to Australia when he was 15 years old.

FARTHING, Arthur Vincent
Arthur was born at Tamworth, NSW where he enlisted on 12th January 1916. He embarked at Sydney on the troopship HMAT 'Clan McGillivray' on 3rd May 1916, serving as 5685, Private, 13th Battalion, Australian Infantry, AIF. Died of a cerebral abscess on 9th November 1916, aged 20. He had been a farm hand. Son of Henry and Jane Farthing of Hercules Street, West Tamworth, New South Wales.

FEILD, Gustav William
Gustav died of pneumonia on 9th November 1918, aged 34. He was born at Murtoa, VIC., Australia, 787, enlisted at Murtoa, embarked at Melbourne on 25th October 1916 on the troopship HMS 'Ulysses'.

At the time of his death he was serving as a Corporal with 3 Squadron Australian Flying Corps. Son of Alfred Francis and Louisa Sarlaw Field of 3 Ascot Street, North Ballarat, Victoria, Australia. He had been a plumber and air mechanic.

FLAHERTY, Patrick Bryan
Pat enlisted at Eton, Queensland on 14th December 1915, embarked on HMAT *'Star of Victoria'* at Sydney on 31st March 1916. He was serving as 5090, Driver, HQ 13th Australian Brigade. He died of influenza on 24th October 1918, aged 29. He had been a labourer. Son of James and Elizabeth Flaherty of North Elton, Mackay, Queensland.

FLETCHER, John Duncan
John was born at Port Chalmers, New Zealand, enlisted at Myrniong, VIC., Australia, on 16th January 1916, embarked on the troopship HMAT *'Suevic'* at Melborne on 21st June 1917. He was serving as 3393, Private, 57th Battalion, Australian Infantry, AIF. He admitted to the City of London Hospital at Clapton on 11th May 1918 and transferred to Harefield on 29th July 1918 where he died of pulmonary catarrh on 12th September 1918, aged 42 (38). He had been gassed in France in April 1918. Son of John and Isabella Fletcher. He had served in the Boer War and was a miner.

GENGE, John Wesley
John was born at Perth, Western Australia, enlisted at Adelaide on 24th February 1917 as 3647, Private, 48th Battalion, Australian Infantry, AIF. He died of a shell wound which had fractured his spine and toxaemia at the hospital on 2nd August 1918, aged 20.

Son of Charles Wesley Genge and Agnes Genge of 103 Hindley Street, Adelaide, South Australia.

GIDDENS, Percy Albert

He enlisted at Kew, VIC., on 18th December 1914, embarking on HMAT *Shropshire* at Melbourne on 20th March 1915. Percy was serving as 1748, Private, 14th Battalion, Australian Infantry, AIF. He died of phthisis (pulmonary tuberculosis) on 1st January 1917, aged 21 or 23. Son of William and Mary Ann Giddens of 54 Derby Street, Kew, Victoria, Australia. He had been a brass finisher.

GRAHAM, Melville Adrian

Melville was born at Cobram, Victoria, where he enlisted on 25th February 1916. He embarked on HMAT *Wandilla* at Melbourne on 6th June 1916 as 12307, Private, 10th Field Ambulance Australian Army Medical Corps. He had been ill but was thought to be improving slightly when he died suddenly of pleurisy and complications on 9th March 1917, aged 25 or 27. Son of John and Annie Graham of 17 Spray Street, Elwood, Melbourne, Victoria, Australia.

GRUBNAU, Michael

Michael enlisted at Laverton, WA., on 13th November 1916 and embarked on HMAT *Persic* at Fremantle on 29th December 1916 as 3152, Private, 46th Battalion, Australian Infantry, AIF. Died of tuberculosis of the lung and middle ear on 23rd June 1918. He had been a stockman. Son of Robert and Mary Grubnau of Coolgardie, Western Australia.

HALL, Charles Samuel

Charles enlisted at Vermont, VIC., on 28th June 1915, embarked on SS *'Makarini'* at Melbourne on 15th September 1915. At the time of his death he was serving as 2606, Sergeant. 14th Battalion, Australian Infantry, AIF. He had been ill for 15 months when he died of tuberculosis of the lungs at Harefield on 22nd June 1917, aged 24. Son of Charles Dawes Hall and Jane Hall of Canterbury Road, Vermont, Victoria, Australia. He was formerly a gardener.

HARTLEY, Frederick Charles

Fred was born at Euroa, Victoria, where he enlisted on 5th February 1915. He embarked on HMAT *'Ceramic'* (a hospital ship which had shuttled back to Australia to take on more reinforcements during the first part of 1915) at Sydney on 25th June 1915. He was serving as 562, Private, 18th Battalion, Australian Infantry, AIF. He was admitted to Tooting Military Hospital suffering from pleurisy and enipyema on 21st June 1917 and transferred to Harefield on 28th June 1917, where he died of enipyema on 24th July 1917, aged 25. Son of John and Alice Maud Hartley of 3 Raglan Street, South Melbourne, Victoria, Australia. He had been a labourer.

HAYDEN, John Arthur

John had enlisted at Delegate, NSW., on 6th January 1916, embarked on HMAT *'Port of Sydney'* at Sydney on 4th September 1916 as 2163, Private, 55th Battalion, Australian Infantry, AIF. Died of cerebro spinal fever on 3rd April 1917, aged 37. Son of James and Elizabeth Hayden of Delegate, New South Wales. He had been a farmer.

HERRON, Edwin George
Enlisting at Launceston, Tasmania, on 23rd March 1915, Edwin embarked on HMAT '*Aeneas*' at Brisbane on 29th June 1915. He served as 1108, Driver, 26th Battalion, Australian Infantry, AIF. After a post-mortem it was shown that he died of influenza, pneumonia and heart failure on 19th October 1918, aged 24 or 26. He had been a labourer. Son of George and May Herron.

HINGST, Leslie Christian
Leslie enlisted at Newcastle, NSW., on 9th November 1915, embarking on HMAT '*Wandilla*' at Sydney on 3rd February 1916, serving as 4514, Private, 1st Australian Pioneers, AIF. Died of a pulmonary tubercle which he had contracted in about November 1916, and exhaustion at Harefield on 26th March 1917, aged 32 (or 33 or 30). He had been a salesman. Son of Henry D. and Susan Hingst; husband of Mary E. Hingst of 41, Havelock Street, Mayfield, Newcastle, New South Wales.

HITCHEN, William Thomas
Born at Mudgee, New South Wales, Will enlisted at Gilgandra, NSW., on 10th October 1915, embarking on HMAT '*Ceramic*' (a hospital ship) at Sydney on 14th April 1916. Will served as 1677, Private. 45th Battalion, Australian Infantry, AIF. He died of melanotic sarcoma on 3rd September 1916, aged 44 or 52. Son of George and Catherine Hitchen; husband of E.J. Hitchen of Bridge Street, Gilgandra, New South Wales, Australia. He was formerly a master plumber and had organized the 'Cooee' march from Gilgandra to Sydney in 1914. As Hitchen's column moved from

town to town, it swelled with volunteers and arrived in Sydney in 1915.

HOBBS, Arthur John

Arthur enlisted at Benalla, NSW., on 6th January 1915, embarked at Melbourne on HMAT 'Wiltshire' on 13th April 1915. 1760, Private, 5th Battalion, Australian Machine Gun Corps. Died of tubercle of the lungs on 26th May 1918, aged 26. He had been wounded in Gallipoli and France. Son of John and Elizabeth Jane Hobbs of Goomalibee Street, Benalla, Victoria, Australia. He was formerly a labourer.

HOGARTH, Joseph

Joe had served in the Boer War as a private and was a grazier. He was born at Wellington Vale, Deepwater, New South Wales, enlisted at Toowoomba, Queensland on 17th June 1915, embarked on HMAT 'Shropshire' at Brisbane on 17th August 1915. 1725, Driver, 26th Battalion, Australian Infantry, AIF. Died of peritonitis on 9th March 1918, aged 39. He had been wounded at Westhoek Ridge during the Third Battle of Ypres between 6th September and 3rd October 1917. Son of William and Ann Cuninghame Hogarth of Balgownie, Cambooga, Queensland.

HOWLETT, James Reuben

James was born in the state of Victoria in Australia, enlisted at Carisbrook on 19th August 1915, embarked on HMAT 'Ceramic' (a hospital ship) at Melbourne on 24th November 1915. 3043, Driver, 5th Field Coy., Australian Engineers. Died of nephritis and anaemia on 2nd June 1917, aged 24. Son of Mr. J. Howlett of Smith Street, Carisbrook, Victoria, Australia.

IVETT, William John
Born at Croydon, South Australia, Will enlisted at Wilkawatt, SA., on 27th September 1915, embarked on HMAT '*Borda*' at Adelaide on 11th January 1916. 1864, Private, Australian Machine Gun Corps, Training Depot, AIF. William died at the hospital of 'lung trouble' (syncope and tubercle of the larynx and lung) on 9th November 1918, aged 30. Son of Joseph and Sarah Ann Ivett of Kent Street, Alberton, South Australia.

JOHNSON, John Stobart
Enlisted at Gosforth, NSW., on 27th September 1915. 5118, Private, 3rd Battalion, Australian Infantry, AIF. He had received gunshot wounds to his spine, probably in operations in the Arras sector, and admitted to the 3rd Australian Casualty Clearing Station at Grevillers on 5th May 1917. He was transferred to Harefield, where he had only been for four days when he died of wounds received 1 month and 17 days previously and descending pyelitis of which he had suffered for 15 days on 22nd June 1917, aged 24. Son of Thomas William and Margaret Ellen Johnson of Fern Hill, Gosford, New South Wales, Australia.

JOHNSTON, Andrew David
Andrew enlisted at Katanning, WA., in 1915, embarked on the troopship HMAT '*Ulysses*' at Fremantle on 1st March 1916. 9446, Private, 4th Field Ambulance Australian Army Medical Corps, AIF. He was injured in his face and mouth and operated on but died five days later of disease (facial erysipelas) at the hospital on 10th February 1917, aged 24 or 25. Only son of Mr. T. Johnston of Timura, Beverley,

Western Australia. He was engaged to be married and was a machine expert and had worked an orderly at the ANZAC Hospital, Harefield.

JONES, Oscar Harold
Born at Oxley, QLD., enlisted at Sherwood, QLD., on 25th September 1915, Oscar embarked at Sydney on 16th February 1916 on the troopship HMAT *'Ballarat'*, a P & O 'B' Class ship built for the Australian service in 1911. The ship was torpedoed and sank on 27th April 1917. He was serving as 8894, Private, 13th Field Ambulance Australian Army Medical Corps. Died of nephritis on 23rd June 1918, aged 25. Son of George Edward Richard and Elizabeth Ann Jones of Oxley, Queensland. He was educated at Brisbane Grammar School and was a clerk.

KEEGAN, Roderick James
Roderick was born at Hamilton, Vic., where enlisted in late March 1916. He embarked on the troopship HMAT *'Ascanius'* at Melbourne on 27th May 1916, serving as 498, Private, 39th Battalion, Australian Infantry, AIF. Died of tuberculosis of the lungs and exhaustion on 20th November 1917, aged 21. Son of John and Ann Keegan of Tyers Street, Hamilton, Victoria, Australia. He had been a coach builder.

KELLY, George Abner
George was born at Boweya and enlisted there on 20th August 1914. He embarked on HMAT *'Suffolk'* at Sydney on 18th October 1914. 185, Private, 2nd Battalion, Australian Infantry, AIF. Died of a liver abscess on 17th April 1916, aged 32. His remains were conveyed to the Churchyard in a glass hearse

accompanied by a Military Band. Son of William and Lucinda Kelly of Boweya, Victoria, Australia.

KELLY, John Patrick

John was born at Nar-Nar-Goon, VIC., where he enlisted on 10th March 1916. He had embarked on HMAT '*Miltides*' at Melbourne on 1st August 1916. 5388, Gunner, 14th Brigade, Australian Field Artillery. He was admitted to the hospital at Harefield Park on 4th October 1918 from the 1st Birmingham War Hospital, and died of a duodenal ulcer on 26th October 1918, aged 39. He had served for about 7 years in the British Army in India and had also been wounded in France. Son of James Egan Kelly and Maria Fahey Kelly and husband of Mary Jane Kelly of 71, Keppell Street, Carlton, Victoria, Australia.

KELLY, Walter

Walter was born at Torrington in Devon. Civilian Australian Munition Worker. He was an Army Pensioner, having served with the Australian Imperial Forces. He died at the hospital of tuberculosis of the kidney and toxaemia on 9th August 1918, aged 48 or 50. Son of Thomas and Grace Kelly of Roborough, Torrington, Devon; husband of Ada Ellen Kelly of 3, Gloucester Road, Croydon.

KEMPF, Thomas Vivian

Tom was born at Daylesford, Victoria. 312, enlisted on 9th March 1916 and embarked on HMAT '*Persic*' at Melbourne on 3rd June 1916. He was a Private with 312 as his service number in the 37th Battalion, Australian Infantry, AIF. Died of phthisis on 27th February 1918, aged 23. He had been a brass finisher.

Son of Charles George Henry and Elizabeth Allen Kempf of 16, Redfern Road, Upper Hawthorn, Victoria, Australia.

KENNEDY, Percy
Percy enlisted at Melbourne on 6th July 1915, serving as 2494, Private. 23rd Battalion, Australian Infantry, AIF. Died of tuberculosis of the lungs on 15th September 1916, aged 18 or 19. Son of Mr. P. Kennedy of Corner of King Street and Little Bourk Street, Melbourne, Australia.

KNELL, Edgar Norman
Born at Malvern, Victoria, Edgar enlisted there on 8th February 1915. He embarked on the troopship HMAT '*Ulysses*' at Melbourne on 10th May 1915, serving as 182, 2nd Corporal, 22nd Battalion Australian Infantry, AIF. Died of stomach cancer and exhaustion at 22, Lucerne Road, Croydon on 15th January 1920, aged 25. Son of Alfred William Knell of 49, Vincent Street, Caulfield East, Victoria, Australia. He had been a farmer (or a labourer). His brother, Victor, was killed in action in the German retreat on 23rd March 1917, aged 23.

KNOX, Leopold Upton (Leslie)
Private Knox was serving as 1562, in the 1st Battalion, Australian Infantry, AIF. He died of wounds at Harefield on 15th November 1916, aged 21. Son of Jaxon Grahme Knox and Annie Knox of Ashfield, Sydney. He had been a mechanic. The 1st Battalion was raised within the first two weeks of war at Randwick near Sidney and sent to Egypt, arriving on December 2nd 1914. From here they went to Gallipoli where they remained until they were

evacuated back to Egypt in December 1915, later going to France where they were first in action at Pozieres in July 1916.

KOOP, Frederick William
Fred enlisted at Horsham, Victoria, on 1st May 1916, embarked on HMAT *'Themistocles'* at Melbourne on 28th July 1916, as 6046, Private, 6th Battalion, Australian Infantry, AIF. Died tuberculosis of the lungs 3.30 on 26th June 1917, aged 25. Son of Frederick Paul and Mary Koop of Lower Norton, Victoria, Australia.

LAKIE, Douglas Vowles
Douglas enlisted at Naracoorte on 18th September 1916, serving as 2944, Lance-Corporal, 50th Battalion, Australian Infantry, AIF. Died of pulmonary tuberculosis on 14th March 1918, aged 19. Son of William and Mary Lakie, of Melbourne, Australia.

LANGE, Leo Julius Edward
Leo was born in South Australia, enlisted at Kojonup, WA., on 13th June 1916, embarked on HMAT *'Miltiades'* at Fremantle on 29th January 1917. 6602, Private (Signaller), 28th Battalion, Australian Infantry, AIF. He died of pulmonary tuberculosis at King George Hospital, Lambeth, on 8th April 1919, aged 21. Son of Rudolph Carl and Frances Lange of Wagin, Western Australia. He had formerly been a mechanic.

LEITCH, William Douglas
Born at Hobart, where William enlisted on 21st May 1915. He embarked on HMAT *'Wandilla'* at

Fremantle on 25th June 1915. At the time of his death he was serving as 2255, Corporal, Australian Army Ordnance Corps, AIF. He died at the No. 3 Auxiliary Hospital, The Orchard Hospital at Dartford from acute miliary tuberculosis, from which he had suffered for about 2 months, and tubercular meningitis which he had suffered from for 9 days, on 4th May 1919, aged 34. Son of William and Jane Leitch of 6 Arthur Street, Hobart, Tasmania; husband of Emma Elizabeth Georgina Leitch of 24 Uamvar Street, St. Leonard's Road, Poplar, London. He had formerly been an engineer. He is buried at Harefield.

LINGLEY, William Lauderdale
William was born at Redland Bay, Queensland, enlisted at Muckadilla, Queensland on 26th September 1916. He embarked on HMAT *'Marathon'* at Sydney on 10th May 1917 as 33736, Gunner, 2nd Div. Ammunition Col. Australian Field Ambulance. He had been admitted to the Fargo Hospital on 11th September 1917 and discharged on 3rd October 1917. He was admitted to the 1st Australian Auxiliary Hospital, Harefield Park on 23rd October 1918 and died of pneumonia on 5th November 1918, aged 27. Son of William and Alice M. Lingley of Muckadilla Hotel, Muckadilla, Queensland.

LITTLE, John Henry
John enlisted at Colo Vale on 7th December 1915, embarked on the hospital ship, HMAT *'Ceramic'* at Sydney on 13th April 1916. He was serving as 4727, Private, 20th Battalion, Australian Infantry. He had received a gunshot wound to his right thigh and left hand and was admitted to Cambridge Military Hospital, Aldershot and later transferred to Harefield

Park on 21st April 1917, where he died from nephritis and heart failure at 3am on 8th June 1917, aged 34. He may have been wounded near Bullecourt on 12th April 1917 in an attack, in the taking of the farming village of Riencourt by the West Australians, New South Welshmen and the Victorians. The attack, which began in the snow on that day had been directed against the line at a point between Bullecourt village on the left and Lagnicourt on the right. The whole front of the attack was on the Hindenburg Line. Son of Mr. C.L. Little of Colo Vale, New South Wales.

LUBY, Reginald
Reg had enlisted at Macleay River, NSW., on 1st June 1916. He embarked on the troopship HMAT '*Ascanius*' at Sydney on 25th October 1916, serving as 2939, Private, 18th Battalion, Australian Infantry, AIF. Died of syncope and pulmonary tuberculosis on 30th September 1918, aged 20. He had been a labourer.

LUCAS, Percival Cecil
Born at Bridgewater, VIC., where he enlisted on 20th June 1916. He embarked on HMAT '*Shropshire*' at Melbourne on 25th September 1916, serving as 2443. Private, 57th Btn., Australian Infantry, AIF. He died of influenza and pneumonia on 10th December 1918, aged 27. Son of Charles and Sarah Lucas of Bridgewater-on-Loddon, Victoria, Australia. He had been a grocer.

LUFF, Charles John
Charles was born at Mount Perry and enlisted there on 24th June 1916 as 2658, Private, 4th Australian

Pioneers. He died of syncope and purulent bronchitis influenza on 25th November 1918, aged 28. Only son of Charles and Margaret Luff of Mount Perry, Queensland. He had formerly been a miner and cane cutter.

MANNS, Thomas Henry
Tom was serving as 2152, Civilian Australian Munition Worker. He died on 9th October 1918, aged 35. He was a discharged Australian soldier who had fought in the war and had been wounded in Gallipoli. He died accidentally while working with Messrs. Higgs and Hill as a tree-feller at Hillingdon Park House. He was sawing off a branch from an oak tree when a bough snapped and hit the ladder on which he was standing. He fell about 40 feet to the ground on his chest. He was taken to Uxbridge Cottage Hospital where he died at 3.45am the same day He is buried in the Churchyard of St. Mary's at Harefield.

MARSHALL, Frederick John William
Fred had enlisted at North Melbourne on 19th October 1916, embarking on HMAT *'Shropshire'* at Melbourne on 11th May 1917. He served as 3307, Driver, 3rd AFA Bde., Australian Field Artillery. Died of pneumonia on 3rd December 1918, aged 22. Son of Frederick and Christina Ann Marshall of 149 Northcote Road, Armadale, Victoria, Australia.

McCALLA, John Thomas
John enlisted on 4th October 1916 and embarked on HMAT *'Kyarra'* (at some time a hospital ship) at Brisbane on 17th November 1916, serving as 2625, Private, 41st Battalion, Australian Infantry, AIF. Died

of sickness on 25th May 1919. Son of Peter Gilbraith McCalla and Mary McCalla of Queensland.

McCARTHY, James Desmond

Enlisted at Ashfield, NSW, James embarked on HMAT *'Argyllshire'* at Sydney on 11th May 1916. He was serving as 18707, Driver, 7th Bde., Australian Field Artillery. He was taken ill in about August 1917 and died of tuberculosis of the lungs and exhaustion on 2nd November 1917, aged 32. Son of Daniel Joseph and Mary Jane McCarthy of Ashfield, Sydney, New South Wales.

McCULLOUGH, Reginald Joseph

Reg was born at Bendigo, Victoria where he enlisted on 15th November 1915. He embarked on HMAT *'Anchises'* on 16th March 1916 at Adelaide. 2203, Gunner, 14th Bde., Australian Field Artillery. Died of eczema and syncope on 30th December 1919, aged 25. Son of Joseph and Elizabeth McCullough of Goyne Road, Epsom, Victoria.

McDONALD, James

James was born at Hay, NSW., enlisted at Ingelwood, Queensland, on 3rd October 1916. He embarked on HMAT *'Beltana'* at Sydney on 25th November 1916 as 3398, Private, 4th Australian Pioneers. Died of enteric on 2nd January 1919, aged 33. Son of James and Isabella McDonald of Ingelwood Post Office, Queensland. He had been a stockman.

MACDONALD, Norman

Norman was born at Port Melbourne, Australia, enlisted on 5th July 1915. He embarked on HMAT *'Nestor'* at Melbourne on 11th October 1915. He was serving as 3343, Private, 21st Battalion, Australian Infantry. He died of chronic nephritis and lobar pneumonia on 24th September 1918, aged 22. Son of James and Elizabeth Macdonald of Beach Road, Black Rock, Victoria. Previously a carter. He had been wounded in France.

MACKAY, Hugh Grant
Born at Carlton, Victoria and enlisted at Fairfield, Victoria on 17th July 1915. 2743, Private, 21st Btn., Australian Infantry, AIF. Died of tubercular peritonitis on 25th July 1918, aged 20. Son of Daniel Grant Mackay and Mary J. Mackay of Templeton Street, Maldon, Victoria, Australia. He had been a farm hand.

MENZIE, Frederick Bertram
Fred was born at New Norfolk, Tasmania where he enlisted on 12th June 1916. He embarked on HMAT *'Botanist'* at Melbourne on 24th August 1916 as 6315, Private, 12th Battalion, Australian Infantry, AIF. He died of tuberculosis of a lung, on 7th September 1917, aged 22. Son of Frederick and Martha Menzie. He had been a farm labourer.

MICKELS, James Henry
James was born at Newcastle, England, enlisted at South Melbourne on 29th September 1915. He embarked on HMAT *'Demosthenes'* at Melbourne on 29th December 1915. 3560, Private, 60th Battalion, Australian Infantry. He had been wounded by gunshot in his right hip at Pozieres in the fighting with the 16th Bavarian Reserve Infantry Regiment (in which Adolf Hitler was serving as a private) and nine months later died of wounds, colitis and exhaustion

from which he had been suffering for several days at Harefield Park, on 20th March 1917, aged 32. The Australians fought at Pozieres from July 1916 and by 8th August 1916, Australian operations around the village had been completed with heavy casualties. After having captured enemy trenches, they had been subjected to counter-attacks and horrendous shelling. Son of James and Sadie Mickels of 328 Park Street, South Melbourne, Victoria, Australia. He had emigrated to Australia with his parents when he was about 9 years old.

MOFFATT, Mervyn Francis
Mervyn was an orderly at the hospital. He had enlisted at North Sydney, NSW., on 30th August 1915 as 13810, Private, Australian Medical Corps. Died of meningitis on 10th October 1916, aged 19. Son of Benjamin and Maria Moffatt of 58 Burlington Street, Crow's Nest, Sydney, New South Wales.

MOORE, Horace William George
Horace enlisted at Bentleigh, Victoria, on 31st January 1916, serving as 267, Private, 59th or 39th Battalion, Australian Infantry, AIF. He died at the Queen Alexandra Military Hospital in London on 26th June 1919, aged 31.A post-mortem was performed which found that he had died from Weil's Disease (toxaemic jaundice), which was mainly caused by rats. Husband of E.R. Moore of 53 Ranelagh Road, Pimlico, London. He is buried at Harefield.

MOORE, Joseph Tregellis
Born at Brighton, Victoria, enlisted at Bendigo, Victoria, on 6th July 1915. He embarked on HMAT 'Nestor' at Melbourne on 11th October 1915. 5802,

Gunner, 106th Howitzer Brigade, 6th Bde., Australian Field Artillery. He was admitted to the hospital on 11th November 1918, suffering from influenza, where he died of influenza and pneumonia on 27th November 1918, aged 21. Son of Edmund Notley Moore and Josephine Moore.

NAYLOR, John
John was British born, and enlisted at Barkstead, Victoria on 18th January 1916. He embarked on HMAT '*Wiltshire*' on 7th March 1916 at Melbourne. 4189, Private, 2nd Battalion, Australian Cyclist Corps. On 25th October 1918 he was admitted to the 9th General Hospital with a compound fracture of the tibia caused by gunshot. He was transferred to Reading War Hospital on 5th November 1917 (?1918?), where he progressed favourably. He died of influenza and double pneumonia at Harefield on 9th November 1918, aged 21. One of their last engagements had been on 3rd October 1918 in an attack on the Beaurevoir line, including the village of Beaurevoir. It had been a day of desperate fighting. Son of John and Mary Naylor of Barkshead, Victoria, Australia.

NOBLE, George Franklin
George had enlisted at Grange, SA., on 19th January 1915, embarked on HMAT '*Wandilla*' at Melbourne on 7th March 1916, serving as 4754, Private, 8th Field Ambulance Australian Army Medical Corps. He was admitted to the hospital where he died of influenza and pneumonia on 13th November 1918. Son of John B. and Amelia Frances Noble of High Street, Grange, South Australia. His younger brother, Alan, serving

with the 10th Battalion, Australian Infantry, AIF, had died of wounds in France on 9th May 1917.

OSBORNE, William Lyle
William was born at Sedgwick, enlisted at Bendigo, Victoria on 14th January 1915. He embarked as a private with the 8th Light Horse Regiment at Melbourne, sailing on HMAT '*Uganda*'. He later served as 982, Sergeant, 11th Bde., Australian Field Artillery. Died from diabetes at 4.45am on 28th August 1917, aged 21 or 23. Son of Ernest Halbert and Christina Osborne of Sedgwick, Bendigo, Victoria, Australia. He had previously been a wardsman in a hospital.

POWER, Leo Joseph
Leo was born at Branxholme, Victoria, where he enlisted on 8th May 1915. He embarked on HMAT '*Demosthenes*' at Melbourne on 16th July 1916 as 2437, Private, 67th Battalion, Australian Infantry, AIF. Died of pericarditis on 31st July 1917, aged 21. Son of Patrick and Ellen Power of Branxholme, Victoria, Australia.

REGAN, Thomas
Tom enlisted at Camperdown on 26th September 1914, embarked on HMAT '*Star of Victoria*' at Melbourne on 25th February 1915. At the time of his death he was serving as 196, Sergeant, 8th Australian Light Horse, AIF. Died at Harefield from phthisis and cardiac failure on 2nd July 1916, aged 27. Father Octavin, of the Catholic Church at Rickmansworth, officiated. Son of Mr. W.R. Regan of Watson Street, Camperdown, Victoria, Australia.

RICHARDS, Albert Stanley
Albert was born at Blaklava, South Australia, enlisted at Owen, SA., on 2nd March 1916, embarked on HMAT *'Seang Bee'* at Adelaide on 13th July 1916. 2016, Corporal, 48th Battalion, Australian Infantry, AIF. Wounded in a desperate fight at Bullecourt on about 12th April 1917. In about September 1917 he contracted tuberculosis of the lungs and died on 1st December 1917, aged 22. The post-mortem discovered he had died of tuberculosis of the lungs and cachexia.He had been a draper. Son of Albert Henry and Annie Richards of Owen, South Australia.

RILEY, William Michael
William was serving as 4558, Private, 9th Battalion, Australian Infantry, AIF. He died at the hospital on 20th June 1918, aged 32. A post-mortem was carried out and it was found that he had died from tuberculosis of the lungs. Son of Thomas and Elizabeth Ann Riley of 48 Orion Street, Lismore, New South Wales.

ROBINSON, Raymond
Ray enlisted at Wingham, NSW., on 16th July 1915, embarked at Sydney on the troopship HMAT *'Euripides'* on 2nd November 1915. 2896, Bombardier, 5th Div. Bde., 10th Australian Trench Mortar Bty, AIF. Died of influenza and pneumonia on 13th November 1918, aged 23 or 25. Son of John and Jane Robinson of Marlee, New South Wales.

ROWLANDS, Cecil Rupert
Cecil enlisted at Currawang, NSW., on 1st September 1914, embarked as a Private on HMAT *'Argyllshire'* at Sydney on 18th October 1914, later serving as 323

(or 325), Gunner, 1st Bde., Australian Field Artillery. Died of jaundice on 20th July 1916, aged 24 or 26. Son of Richard and Emily D. Rowlands of Currawang, Goulburn, New South Wales.

RUGG, Frederick
Fred was born at Sydney and enlisted at Petersham, NSW., on 18th July 1915. He embarked on the troopship HMAT *'Euripides'* at Sydney on 2nd November 1915.At the time of his death he was serving as 2805, Corporal, 56th Battalion, Australian Infantry, AIF. Wounded in the head by shrapnel at Proyart in France between 16th and 18th August 1918 and admitted to No.5 RAMC General Hospital, Rouen on 19th August 1918. He was transferred to the 1st London Hospital on 8th September 1918 and operated on five days later to remove a foreign body from the jura and was further operated on 1st October 1918. He was admitted to the hospital, where he died of a cerebral abscess on 11th December 1918, aged 25. Son of James Frederick and Alice Rugg of 3R, Church Street, Marrickville, Sydney, New South Wales. He was an optician.

SCOTT, George Alexander
George was born at North Fitzroy and enlisted at Colac, Victoria, on 11th February 1915. He embarked on the troopship HMAT *'Ulysses'* at Melbourne on 10th May 1915. 897, Private, 22nd Battalion, Australian Infantry. He received multiple leg wounds in action at Bapaume during the Second Battle of the Somme and was admitted to the 6th General Hospital on 23rd March 1917. He was transferred to the 1st London General Hospital on 17th April 1917 where his right leg was amputated through the thigh. By 21st

April 1917 the wound had gone septic. He had a further operation on about 9th May 1917 and on 21st July 1917 was transferred to Harefield, where he died of septicemia and pyamaeia on 9th December 1917, aged 22. Son of James and Annie Scott of North Fitzroy, Victoria, Australia. He had been a farmer.

SETON, Miles Charles Cariston
Major Seton, Australian Army Medical Corps stationed at the Australian Auxiliary Hospital, Harefield. He had been stationed at Harefield since 26th November 1918. He was shot dead in the drawing room at 13 Clarendon Road, Holland Park the home of his cousin, Sir Malcolm Seton on 13th January 1919, aged 44. At his trial, his assailant Colonel Rutherford was found 'guilty but insane'. Major Seton was born in Edinburgh where he took his medical degrees and afterwards practiced in Melbourne. He had joined the Australian Medical Corps as Captain in December 1915. He left Australia for Egypt in the hospital ship '*Kanowna*' on 22nd December 1915. After service in Egypt he came to England in 1916 and had served at several depots and camps before arriving at Harefield. His coffin was conveyed in an Australian ambulance by a party of the Australian Imperial Forces to the London Necropolis. Four officers and six privates from the Australian Auxiliary Hospital at Harefield acted as bearers. He is not commemorated locally. Buried: Brookwood Military Cemetery, Surrey.

SHARP, Oswald Graham, MSM
Oswald was born at Castlemaine, Victoria, Australia, enlisted at Hawthorn, Victoria in late August 1915. He embarked as a Bombardier on HMAT '*Wiltshire*'

at Melbourne on 18th November 1915. 6420, Battery QMS., 4th Brigade Australian Field Artillery. He died of apoplexy on 10th April 1919, aged 49. He had been a clothing manufacturer. Son of Walter Sharp and Margaret Summerscates his wife. He had been awarded the Meritorious Service Medal.

SHIRLAW, Hugh William

Hugh was born at Bathurst, New South Wales, where he enlisted on 22nd February 1916, serving as 5410, Private, 20th Battalion, Australian Infantry, AIF. Died of facial erysipelas on 9th December 1918, aged 37. Son of Mrs. Jane Shirlaw.

SMITH, Bert

Bert was born at Oakland and enlisted at Coraki on 25th September 1915. He embarked as a Private at Sydney, sailing on HMAT 'Star of Victoria' on 31st March 1916. 5196, Corporal, 49th Australian Infantry, AIF. Died of chloroform asphyxia and cardiac failure on 18th July 1917, aged 22. Son of Ernest John and Sarah Ann Smith of Oakland, Richmond River, New South Wales.

SMITH, Clement

Clem was born at Mintaro, South Australia, enlisted at Morgan, South Australia. He embarked on the troopship HMAT 'Suevic' as a driver, at Adelaide on 31st May 1916. At the time of his death he was serving as 9671, Lance-Cpl., 11th Field Coy., Australian Engineers. Died of suppurating hydatid of the liver and heart failure on 31st December 1918, aged 31 or 32. Son of James Stewart and Sarah Jane Smith; husband of Myra A. Smith of Strathalbyn, South Australia.

SNADDEN, Robert Showers
Robert was born at Fitzroy where he enlisted on 26th July 1915, serving as 1931, Private, 3rd Australian Pioneers. Died of a tubercle lung on 30th May 1917, aged 24. Son of Joseph Lander Snadden and Jane Price Snadden of Fitzroy, Melbourne, Australia.

STEVENS, Charles Edward
Charles enlisted at Tragiwel, Victoria, on 22nd August 1914. He embarked at Melbourne on 19th on the troopship HMAT *'Hororata'* and served as 834, Private, 7th Battalion, Australian Infantry, AIF. Wounded at some time and contracted tuberculosis five months before he died of tuberculosis of the lungs on 26th June 1917, aged 24. His younger brother, Sidney Frederick Stevens, was born at 114, Windmill Road, Croydon, on 23rd August 1887. He was educated at Sydenham Road School, probably as Charles had been, and was killed in action in the trenches at Ypres on 20th September 1916, whilst serving as a sergeant in the 2nd Royal Fusiliers. He was one of a party who raided the German trenches at 2am. The raid was unsuccessful. He was the only one killed and five were wounded. They were the sons of Matilda Stevens of 114 Windmill Road, Croydon, England and the late George Stevens.

SUTHERLAND, William John
William was born at Coolah, New South Wales, enlisted at Charters Towers, Queensland on 29th September 1916. He embarked on HMAT *'Persic'* at Fremantle on 29th December 1916 as 3196, Private, 4th Australian Pioneers. He died of diabetes on 23rd April 1918, aged 35. Son John and Kate Sutherland;

husband of Emma Louisa Sutherland of Ismail Street, Avr, Queensland.

TAYLOR, Arthur John
Arthur was born at Port Adelaide, South Australia, enlisted at Stirling West, SA on 22nd September 1915. He embarked on HMAT '*Miltiades*' at Adelaide on 7th February 1916. 4585, Private, 10th Battalion, Australian Infantry, AIF. Died of illness on 10th (or 16th) July 1916, aged 35. He had been a butcher.

TEAKEL, Clarence
Clarence was serving as 2464, Private, 30th Battalion, Australian Infantry, having enlisted at Myrtleford, Victoria, on 15th July 1915. He was admitted to the hospital suffering from a severe skin disease where he contracted pneumonia and died from broncho pneumonia and dermatitis, on 2nd October 1918, aged 23. Son of Charles William and Elizabeth Teakel of Myrtleford, Victoria, Australia.

THORNTON, Mervyn Willoughby
Mervyn was born at Sydney, New South Wales, enlisted at Drummoyne on 5th August 1915. He embarked on HMAT '*Nestor*' at Sydney on 9th April 1916 as 10088, Private, 14th Field Ambulance, Australian Army Medical Corps. Died of influenza, broncho-pneumonia and syncope on 30th October 1918, aged 24. Son of Sydney James and Sarah Ellen Thornton of 'Glenwood', Queenscliff, Manby, New South Wales. He was a student. His brother Charles, also serving as a Private in the Australian Army Medical Corps, 14th Field Ambulance, was killed at Polygon Wood, Ypres, on 21st September 1917.

TOUCHELL, Thomas Daniel

Tom was serving as 343 (or 434), Signalman., HMAS *'Kent'*, Royal Australian Navy (Naval Reserve). Died at the No. 2 Australian Auxiliary Military Hospital at Norwood (Southall) of influenza from which he had suffered for 7 days and pneumonia which he had had for 5 days, on 11th April 1919, aged 19. Son of Thomas John Touchell, who also served during the war, and Lucy Janet Touchell of 114 Marmion Street, Fremantle, Western Australia. His death certificate names him as E.W. Touchell.

TUCK, William

William enlisted at Flinders, Vic., on 30th December 1915 as 759, Private, 41st Battalion, Australian Infantry, AIF. He embarked on HMAT *'Demosthenes'* at Sydney on 18th May 1916. Died of an amoebic abscess of the liver and emphysema, with which he had suffered for two weeks, on 13th (or 18th) April 1917, aged 35 or 37. Son of Henry and Margaret Jane Tuck of Flinders, Victoria, South Australia. He had been a labourer.

WAKE, Robert Sidney

Robert was born at Cullercoats, Northumberland, England, lived at Melbourne, enlisted at Sydney, NSW., on 19th August 1914. He embarked on HMAT *'Orvieto'* at Port Melbourne on 18th May 1916, serving as 170, Private, 5th Battalion, Australian Infantry, 2nd Brigade, AIF. He had been wounded at Gallipoli and died of wounds (carcinoma of the rectum, cachexia and heart failure) on 8th February 1916, aged 22 (or 23 or 24). Son of James and Margaret Jane Wake. Formerly a ship's steward, he had emigrated to Australia at the age of 18.

WALTON, Charles

Charles enlisted at Adelaide on 6th September 1916, embarking on the troopship HMAT '*Afric*' at Adelaide on 6th November 1916. He was serving as 3004, Private, 50th Battalion, Australian Infantry, AIF. He died of secondary anaemia (post diphtheritic), asphyxia and oedema glottidis on 10th August 1918, aged 29. Brother of Mrs. A.G. Gneath of Robe, South Australia.

WARING, Frederick Charles Macleod

Frederick was born at Hamilton, Victoria where he enlisted on 4th September 1915. He embarked on HMAT '*Wiltshire*' at Melbourne on 18th November 1915. At the time of his demise he was serving as 9339, Corporal, Australian Army Postal Corps. He had been admitted to the Endell Street Military Hospital at Covent Garden in London on 10th April 1919 where he died of septicaemia at 6.30am on 19th May 1919, aged 27. Formerly 42nd Battery, 11th Bde Australian Field Artillery. Son of Murdock Saxeby Waring and Caroline Waring of 145 Kooyony Road, Toorak, Victoria, Australia. He had been a banker with the Bank of Australia.

WEST, Charles Herbert

Charles was born at Rockhampton, Queensland on 29th October 1915. He embarked on HMAT '*Borda*' at Sydney on 5th June 1916. At the time of his death from asphyxia, pneumonia and influenza at Harefield on 6th November 1918, he was serving as 978, Sergeant, 42nd (or 41st) Australian Infantry, AIF. He was aged 22 years. Son of Mr. G.F. West of Mount Morgan, Queensland, Australia.

WILKINSON, William

William was born at Burnley, England, enlisted at Southport, Queensland, on 25th October 1916. He embarked on HMAT *'Wiltshire'* at Sydney on 7th February 1917 as 4923, Private, Australian Imperial Force HQ. He died of sickness on 2nd May 1919, aged 23. Son of Jeremiah and Sarah Hannah Wilkinson of Gregory Street, Auchinflower, Brisbane, Australia. His family had emigrated to Australia when he was 14 years old. His comrades considered him a genius at music.

SELECT BIBLIOGRAPHY

ADAMS-SMITH, P. The Anzacs. Hamish Hamilton, 1978

BEAN, C.E.W. The Australian Imperial Force in France and the Allied offensive, 1918. Angus and Robertson, 1942

BRITTON, T. Harefield in World War One. 2nd edition, 2013

DOYLE, A.C. The British Campaigns in Europe 1914-1918. Geoffrey Bles, 1928

The Great War: the standard history of the all-Europe conflict, edited by H.W. Wilson. The Amalgamated Press Limited, various volumes 1916-1921

Harefield Park Boomerang. No date, privately printed.

The Middlesex County Times (various dates)

ROGERS, H.C.B. Troopships and their history. Seely Service & Co., 1963

SHEPHERD, M. The Heart of Harefield. Quiller Press, 1990